How Willy Got His Wings

By
Deborah Turner
Diana Mohler

Illustrated by Susan Ahrend

Illustrations by Susan Ahrend
Cover and Interior layout by The Printed Page, Phoenix, AZ
This book was created in CorelDraw 10.

Published by Doral Publishing, Inc., Phoenix, AZ
www.doralpub.com

Printed in China

ISBN: 0-944875-88-2

I dedicate this book to:

my best friend

my mom

Norma Kaye Kramer

Whose insights

Continue to teach me everyday

About compassion, acceptance of others,

How to love without expectation

That life is a daily gift to be cherished

That we should have courage,

Because there is hope

We should have faith

Because there are angels in our company.

Sometimes they are hard to recognize

Since they don't always have wings.

Some move amidst us

With a set of wheels.

—Deborah Turner

This book is dedicated to my family,
which keeps growing.
They are the joy in my life.
It is also dedicated to my good friends
who keep me thinking and evolving.
And to Sarge, my dog, who makes me laugh.

—Diana Mohler

" BZZZZZZZzzzzzz!!"

"Already?" Willy groaned to himself. Morning had come much too quickly. It seemed as though he had just closed his eyes when the alarm clock was telling him that it was time to wake up. He peeked one shiny little eye out of the covers and looked at the noisy clock.

"Six o'clock? Why, it's still dark outside. How can we fly in the airplane if it's dark out?" he wondered. Well, maybe this was good. Maybe they couldn't fly if it was still dark.

Getting on an airplane to fly all the way to Florida scared Willy so much that he had a big knot right in the middle of his stomach. He swallowed to make it go away, but it stayed right there.

Deborah, his mom, was so excited about the trip that she'd been up for hours getting ready. From under the safety of his covers, Willy watched her as she hurried from suitcase to suitcase. Sweet Pea, the other family Chihuahua, had tried to scare him yesterday by telling him that Deborah was going to pack him in a suitcase. When Sweet Pea saw the look in Willy's eyes, he couldn't keep a straight face, and he fell over laughing.

"Come on, Willy, don't look so scared," Deborah said when she saw him peering at her. "It'll be an adventure, you'll see. We're going to meet your grandparents and their little dog, Chiquita. It'll be like you're Superman. Up, up, and awaaaaay…"

Her voice trailed off as she walked down the hall to brush her teeth.

Willy was excited about meeting his new grandparents. Or at least he thought he was. He really wanted them to like him, but…what if they didn't? If they didn' t like him, would Deborah send him away?

He really didn't want to go back to the hospital where Deborah had found him. He liked it here. There was that knot in his stomach again.

Willy could hardly believe that he had lived here with Deborah and the other animals for only months instead of years.

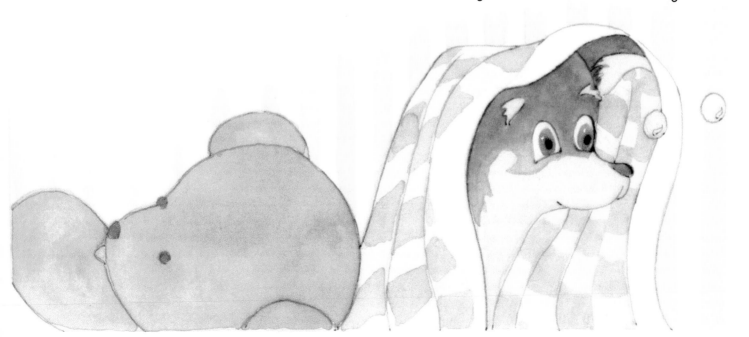

He thought back to the kind doctor
who had found him, and the animal hospital where he lived
before Deborah adopted him. He remembered the day Deborah
brought him home and how she had tied balloons around his waist
to try to help him walk. Instead of walking, he'd actually floated
right off the ground because he was so small.

His favorite memory, though, was the day the truck brought
a big box addressed to him. Inside was a shiny, new wheelchair.
The past months had been heaven, and now that Willy had his bike
There wasn't anything he couldn't do.

"Except fly," he thought. "I sure don't have any wings."

Deborah came back in and put him in his wheelchair, buckling his straps. "I might not have any wings," he said, "but I can sure run!" Willy raced into the kitchen, hoping Marshmallow, the cat, had left a little food in her bowl.

"Bing-bong!" the doorbell rang. The bright yellow taxi had come to take them to the airport. Deborah opened the door and gave a tall man the large flowery suitcase. "We'll be right out," she said. Willy watched with fascination as the man wheeled the suitcase out of the door and hoisted it into the car. He was discovering wheels on many things and couldn't help thinking they were the greatest invention ever. Boys rode by on bicycles, pulling wagons, jumping the curbs with skateboards (that thought made him shiver remembering his harrowing encounter with a skateboard). It appeared that people attached wheels to everything.

With his head lowered, Willy slowly walked
around the room. "Goodbye, Marshmallow."
"Mrrrow." Marshmallow, the fluffy white
Persian cat, jumped onto her windowsill and
pretended to be busy with tidying her perfect hair.
"You lucky dog," Willy said to Sweet Pea.
"You get to stay home."
Sweet Pea rolled his eyes. "I'm not lucky.
The pet sitter's coming to take care of me,
and she's a bad cook. She has scary purple hair and,"
he lowered his voice to a whisper, "she even talks to herself.
I'd much rather be flying. I wouldn't be afraid."

"It's not just the plane…" Willy started to say.

Honk…honk!

The taxi driver was
growing impatient.
The pet nanny had just arrived
—purple hair and all—
and Deborah, leaned over, kissed them all,
then scolded Sweet Pea.
"I expect you to behave."

Beep! Beep!!
"Let's hurry, Willy!"
Before he could tell Sweet Pea
what he'd really meant to say or tell everyone
how much he'd miss them, Deborah scooped him
up and, pulling another suitcase behind her,
ran to the waiting vehicle.
As the car pulled away the knot in Willy's stomach
grew larger. He gulped again to try to make it
go away, but it refused to budge.
The impatient taxi driver
made Willy feel even more nervous.
Honk…honk…honk…
the people in the crosswalk jumped out of his way.
Finally, the tires screeched as the taxi swerved
to the curb at the airport. "Whew…I sure am glad
that we arrived here in one piece,"
Deborah whispered to Willy.
Willy licked her on the nose
to show her he agreed.

"Now, stay right there, Willy,
while I grab that cart for our suitcases."
Willy felt tiny next to the luggage
that towered beside him.

The airport was bustling with people,
policemen with whistles directing traffic,
children, and noise—
lots and lots of noise.
Over it all, he could hear planes
roar down the runways
before they leaped into the air.

Very soon, he knew, he'd be on one of those.

Willy looked up
at the crowd of strangers
that had formed around him.
"Would you look at that!"
The surprised man towered over Willy.
"Oh my!" said the lady with him. "What's the story there?"
"What happened to **him**?" came another curious voice from the crowd.
Maybe they didn't mean it the way it sounded, but something in their tone made Willy feel like he was really different, and his spirits sunk back into his toes. All he wanted to do was get away, but he couldn't move because this circle of feet completely surrounded him.

He was glad to hear her familiar voice. "It's a wheelchair," Deborah said, trying to answer some of their questions. "I'm sorry, but we're running late.
Now keep up with me, Willy."

Deborah and Willy made their way into the terminal
through the throngs of bustling people. There were legs everywhere…
a forest of legs.
What shoes was Deborah wearing?
Were they red? Blue? Or were they her white sneakers?
Willy dodged in and out of people. "Mom! Mom! Wait up!"
"Your tickets, ma'am?" the agent said and pointed the way to the elevator.

Aha!
Here was something
he finally recognized.
He knew what an elevator
was from their trips to
the children's hospital.
    In fact, he was practically
an elevator expert.
Well, he would be if he
could reach the buttons.
It was nice to have
something he recognized.

As they waited for the elevator to arrive,
another crowd of onlookers gathered around them.
                    "Is he a toy? Battery controlled?"
            A little boy kneeled down to get a better look. "What's wrong with him?"
        "Nothing's wrong with me," Willy wanted to say, "I'm fine the way I am."

Ding...

The elevator doors slid open. Willy sighed with relief, as he got in,
leaving Deborah to politely answer the questions.
He looked up at all of the buttons way above him,
and he felt the elevator tremble.
He knew that meant the doors would close any second.

Willy looked from the buttons to Deborah
and back again.
"Hurry, Mom, hurry!"
"I'm coming...
Sir, would you please hold that door?"

But before she could get into the elevator,
the doors slammed closed.

Willy blinked as the car
rose up to the third floor.
What to do…what to do…
Should he stay there and
ride back down or
                    should he get out?
Before he could decide,
the car jerked to a stop, and
                    the doors opened.

Willy—wondering how Deborah would find him—walked out.

"Dad, look at that little dog!" said a young girl in a
wheelchair. Other people stopped and stared, too.

Following the crowd of people walking down the hall,
Willy thought that maybe they knew the way to the
airplane. That's it! Deborah would have to go to the
airplane, so that was the best place to find her.

"Attention..." a booming voice filled the entire terminal. "There is a small dog on wheels lost in the airport. If anyone finds a Chihuahua on wheels, please report to the ticket counter." Willy couldn't believe his ears. How about that? There was another dog just like him, with wheels and everything, lost in the airport! "Maybe I am not so strange after all." He looked around. Wherever that little dog was, Willy sure would like to meet him. Well, right now, it didn't matter. He had to find Deborah. The girl in the wheelchair behind him said, "Hey, Dad! I think that's the little dog that's lost. We should follow him." She pushed her chair after Willy as fast as she coul. "Lost?" Willy thought. "I'm not lost, I know exactly whe I'm heading. The airplane and Deborah are this way— or, well, at least I hope they are."

Willy raced past a couple with their baby in a stroller. "Poor dog! He's lost. Let's try to catch him."

"No, no, no..". Willy thought. "I'm not the one that's lost. That's some other dog." But the parents followed him anyway.

He ran past a skycap with a big, bristly beard. "Hey, little dog, they're looking for you. Stop!"

Hanging onto his cart, the skycap bounded after Willy.

"Not me!" Willy thought. "Is this hallway ever going to end? Where's the airplane? What kind of crazy airport is this if it doesn't have any airplanes?"

"Whoa, dude!" said a teenage boy with long hair. His in-line skates were tossed over one shoulder by knotted laces.

"Wow...I'm totally impressed. That little dog is fast!"
e struggled to pull on his skates so that he could catch
p with the small dog.

Willy ducked into the corner bookstore. He nearly ran into the clerk, who was unloading his bookcart onto the shelves. "There is a small dog on wheels lost in the airport! If anyone finds him, please contact airport security!" The book clerk was so shocked to see Willy that he dropped his armload of books. He tried to quickly maneuver his cart into the aisle to corner the tiny dog, but the spilled books blocked the passage.

Willy turned and ran the opposite way. He followed the maze of aisles up and down, back and forth…and finally, out of the store back into the crowd of people. They were all pushing in one direction, toward a row of arched doorways.

"Your attention, please. A small dog named Willy is lost in the airport!"

Oh no! Deborah must think **he's** lost. He really had to find her.

Artist's Name

Date

19

The crowd slowed.
They waited in a long line
as Willy ran past. He pushed
his way through all of the legs
to get through those doorways.

"Maybe Deborah is on
the other side waiting for me,"
he hoped as he bolted
through the door.

Bing Bing Bing Bing Bing Bing Bing!

Willy froze in his tracks as
the alarms screamed.
"Did *I* do that?"
"The dog set off the security
alarms," he heard the whisper pass
from person to person.

A big, very serious man in uniform
raced toward him. "Hmm, what did you do to set off
the alarm?" he asked.

"It's his wheelchair," said the little girl, who caught up with him.
She smiled at Willy.

"He's got wheels," said the skycap with the bristly beard. "That's the dog they've been looking for. His wheelchair must be made of metal and it set off the alams."

Willy's eyes widened, and his ears flattened. The man in uniform scooped him up and placed him on the table. Everyone stopped what they were doing and watched. He took a strange wand from his pocket. He waved it over and around Willy.

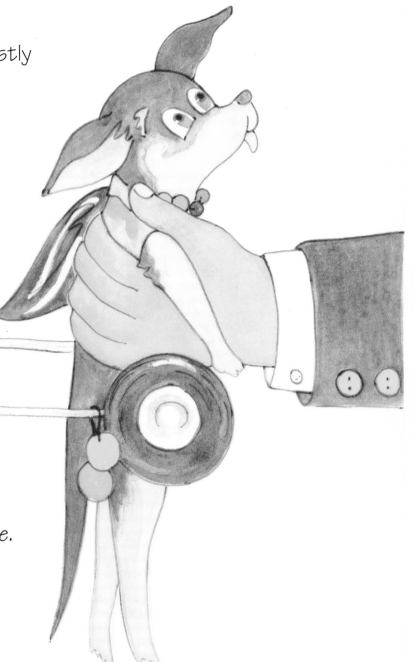

"Wiiiilllllly!"

Deborah rushed through the same arched entrance.
"Is this your dog, lady?" the man in uniform sternly asked.

"Yes," cried Deborah. "Oh, Willy, I was so scared that you were lost."

He blinked his eyes and looked up into Deborah's face. What? Deborah was afraid, too? Did she get an awful knot in her stomach? Maybe being frightened wasn't so strange after all.

Willy looked out at the crowd of worried faces that had followed him. All of these people had only been trying to help him. Suddenly, these strangers just didn't seem like strangers anymore.

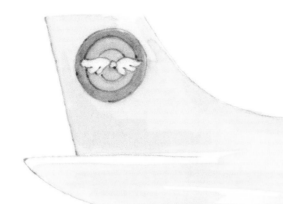

"Ah, well, I guess he's okay." A kind smile began to break on his face. The guard set Willy back on the floor and asked, "So What's with the wheels?"

Thrilled to be united with his mom, Willy marched courageously toward the plane. He noticed that the knot in his stomach was smaller.

"It's just like a bus," he said to himself as they stepped onto the plane. "It's just like a bus, with wings."

"Here's a comfy pillow for you to sit on," the stewardess said, "and a blanket to keep you warm." She put the seat belt over him and buckled the clasp. "Enjoy the flight," she said.

As Willy munched the turkey sandwich that she had brought to him, he saw that some of the people who had chased him were also getting on the airplane. They all smiled at him. "I never saw little feet move so fast," said the boy with the skates.

Willy felt the big airplane begin to move. The engines roared to life, and the whole cabin shook with a feeling of excitement. The plane raced down the runway. "What? Even this big plane has wheels?" He and his mom were drawn to the backs of their seats by the speed of the takeoff. The front of the plane started lifting, like they were going up, up, up a very steep hill. Then, with a small lurch, they were off the runway, and he knew they were in the air.

Artist's Name

Date

25

Willy thought about trying to see out of the windows, but the hum of the engines made him very, very sleepy. "I wonder if the clouds really do look like cotton like Sweet Pea had said?"

The plane made a bump as it touched down. He'd fallen asleep! "Hmm," he thought with a yawn, "flying wasn't so bad at all."

Suddenly, the knot in his stomach was back and bigger than ever as he remembered why they were here...his new grandparents! What if they didn't like him? What if Deborah forgot to tell them about his wheels?

Just then, the flight attendant leaned down and whispered in Deborah's ear, "Can you wait a bit? The captain would like to see Willy in the cockpit. We have something for him."

They waited until everyone else had gotten off and then, this time with Deborah behind him, Willy made his way up the aisle of the airplane where the pilot was waiting for him with a beaming smile.

The captain was a handsome man with gray hair, dressed in a dark blue uniform. Willy was a little surprised when the tall man picked him up, wheels and all, and placed him in the pilot's seat. He even let Willy try on his hat, but it was much too big.

"Willy, I understand you were a little afraid to fly." Willy peeked out from under the captain's hat. "It's okay to be afraid," he said, patting Willy's head. "In fact, when I first started flying, I was afraid, too. But being afraid should should never keep you from doing the things you want to do."

Wow! Even the captain had been afraid of flying? Now he was a pilot and flew all the time. "I think today you earned your wings, Willy," he said. He carefully unpinned a set of wings from his own chest, bent down, and pinned the wings on Willy's shirt. Everyone around him clapped. Willy knew that he didn't need wings to make him feel brave, not anymore.

As Willy and Deborah made their way toward the baggage claim area,
Willy ran ahead. He didn't mind whether people stared or not.
He waited for Deborah at the top of the escalator.

When he looked down into the lobby, Willy saw many of the different
people he'd already met—the little girl in her wheelchair, the parents
with the child in a stroller, the boy carrying his skates—and lots of
other people that he didn't know. They were looking up at him, pointing, and some were waving.
Willy suddenly realized it really didn't matter if you were different. It's who you are
and what you do that matters. What you can do is more important
than what you can't. All these people had been very kind to him,
and that's what he wanted to be to his new grandparents.
And just like that,
the knot in his stomach completely disappeared.
He couldn't make someone like him,
but he could choose to be likeable.

At the bottom of the escalator, Willy saw
a smiling man and woman, both with gray hair.
They looked so much like Deborah
that they just had to be his new grandparents.
In his arms,
the man held a tiny blonde Chihuahua,
whose tail was
wagging
furiously.

Something
about that little dog
reminded him
a lot of Sweet Pea,
and Willy just knew
he was in for one wild vacation.

29